BLURRING EDGES: PICTORIAL ESSAYS ON BORDERS, BUILDINGS, AND A BRATWURST

Blurring Edges:
Pictorial Essays on Borders, Buildings, and a Bratwurst

Linn Song

BORDER
BOOKS
MUNICH

BorderBooks, Munich

Book design by Linn Song
Proof-reading / editing by Marni MacRae

Bibliografische Information der Deutschen Nationalbibliothek:
Die Deutsche Nationalbibliothek verzeichnet diese Publikation in der Deutschen
Nationalbibliografie; detaillierte bibliografische Daten sind im Internet über
http://dnb.d-nb.de abrufbar.

ISBN 978-3-9822477-6-2

CONT

000   Preface • Introduction...01

001   Blurring Edges | (Photos) Europe..05

002   Going Home | Signs..17

003   Proximity | Domesticity...31

004   **Change | Reinvention**...37

005   **Talk to Me | Desertion**..49

006   Territory | Memory...59

007   **How to Defend a Border With a Sausage** | **Roadwork**..................73

008   **In Between | Waiting**..81

009   **Conflict | Landscape**...97

010   Smudges | Crossings...107

011   Notes..119

012   Images...121

0.0.1

PREFACE.
INTRODUCTION

D 39
ALLEMAGNE

It has taken me a ridiculous 15 years to finally finish this small book of pictures and essays. It began as two separate projects, with the book a much larger undertaking of several drafts and more than 250 pages centered around the "politics of 'place'." The photographs, taken more than fifteen years ago with an entry-level consumer digital pocket camera, were part of an initial, exploratory trip over the course of five weeks in two summers, during which I drove through and documented every border-crossing between Germany and its neighbors to the west, beginning from the southern-most border-crossing at Huningue (FR) and Weil-am-Rhein (DE) and ending in Nieuwe Statenzijl where the Westerwoldse Aa river empties into the Dollart Bay and North Sea.

The common theme that ran through both projects was "borders and boundaries," both physical and metaphysical. Although this book is about national borders, borders are also the essence of architecture. It is the moment that separates outside and inside, wet and dry, cold and hot, windy and calm, loud and quiet.

Architecture uses floors, walls and roofs... or undulating planes in today's blob architecture, to define these moments. These architectural elements are then manipulated, and through perforations begin to choreograph moments between dark and light, noisy and calm, heavy and delicate. And as soon as architecture becomes a physical reality e.g., in the form of a wall then it also becomes political. It becomes an exclusionary tool to divide public and private, natural and artificial, dangerous and safe, us and them, and can shape both perceptions and realities.

Due to various reasons, and although under contract, the book project stuttered, stopped, and restarted multiple times over the years. However, as time passed, the topic never left my head because borders are omnipresent not only in architecture, but also in the news and current events of today. Trump's Wall on the US-Mexican border, the Israeli West Bank wall, Ireland, North and South Korea, and the various new walls and fences surrounding the most recent refugee "crisis" in Europe (Austria, Germany, Hungary, the Mediterranean Sea) are just a few of many conflicts involving physical borders and boundaries. Additionally, conflicts "created" by language, laws, politics, and culture in general are strengthening metaphysical borders and divisions between people as they search for protection and security from the "Other."

This "new" project evolved out of the desire to bring the projects to some sort of closure and to "get more mileage" out of the photographs that had been exhibited at Miami University in Oxford, Ohio and the Mockbee Gallery in Cincinnati, since the internal borders of Europe once again became relevant after Syrian and North African refugees began seeking protection in large numbers in Europe in 2015. There continues to be partial internal border closures and controls between Austria and Germany, Hungary, Croatia and Serbia, as well as in the Mediterranean Sea, which are intended to control the flow of refugees into the respective countries. And along with the most recent Coronavirus/Covid-19 pandemic, these actions have fueled ongoing discussions about external and internal borders around and within a "troubled" and increasingly "un-unified" and nationalistic Europe.

The photos and short essays are loosely arranged around 10 ideas about borders, varying in scale from nations and landscapes down to an eight-centimeter-long sausage. A couple of the essays contain ideas and excerpts from the original book, but coupled with the photographs, it became clear that the texts were too long and "academic" in nature to be understood as two types of media with two types of communicative languages that should be working in tandem. The border between text and image is intended to be continually breached, such that the texts add more meaning to the images and vice versa. It seemed logical to use two types of media or "languages" to ponder the topic of physical and imagined borders, and so this book became a hybrid with the intention of using the mixed-media approach to provoke open-ended thought and reflection. The texts and images attempt to expose the often unintended ambiguity of borders and boundaries and to recognize, if not celebrate, the gray over black or white, the "in between" over "here" or "there"... and the blurriness over clarity.

Linn Song

The borders of nations are socially/culturally constructed edges; barriers that psychologically and politically demarcate cultural boundaries and artificially mark territory that does not necessarily have any relationship to the landscape or physical environment. The conditions under which national borders in Europe were "fronts" and centers of conflict and battles over political, cultural, economic, and military power have shifted. In the "new" Europe, cities and the political arena have now become the places and spaces in which disputes over culture, identity, and power arise and are negotiated. Thus, the internal borders of the European Union are slowly transforming into a different kind of space in which the edges have become "fuzzy," bringing with it the potential (or pitfall as many argue?) of melting together "natural," cultivated, built, and acculturated environments.

The photographs in this book are a sampling of the documentation of a changing border between Germany and its neighbors to the west (France and the Benelux countries). The compositions look specifically at the simultaneously abstract and concrete juncture of nations upon which custom/border control edifices once stood or still stand. While these places once "clearly" marked territory, they are now simply remnants of the Schengen Agreement/Aquis (1985/1997), which eliminated the border control points within the European Union. The images are intended to be little "storytellers" — informal snapshots that reveal the scars of conflict and exclusion and, in some cases, the wonderfully subversive acts that unite and heal. These acts range from suppressed voices

being "heard" on graffiti-ed walls to the re-use of abandoned customs complexes for markets featuring local products from both sides of the border. In another particular instance, the purchasing of a border control edifice on the Dutch side and its hard-fought transformation into a single-family home by a binational Dutch-German, married homosexual couple (at the time, same-sex marriage was not recognized in Germany), show how lives literally and figuratively transgress borders on a daily basis.

So, what do border-crossings of nation-states and their documentation have to do with architecture? The point of departure began with my master's thesis on the "politics of building(s)," constructed imagery, representation, and their relationship to identity at multiple scales. For example, as a result of the "Bilbao-Effect"[1] that Frank Gehry's Guggenheim Museum generated, it was becoming apparent that some buildings were becoming something like Hollywood celebrities — their eccentricities celebrated as opposed to being condemned for being/looking different as most new architecture is. The "star-status" of certain architects apparently gave them the "authority" to create "UFOs" in places, just as historically, the ruling nobility and Church gave "justification" for erecting monuments of their power with their own architectural highlights. Aggressively unique architecture was taking on an important role as a tool in helping drive the 21st century tourist economy and the engagement of internationally acclaimed "star" architects was essential in appeasing an otherwise skeptical and "emotionally critical" public. The standard process that unfolded in Bilbao has been replayed all over the world, time and time again: proposal > rejection > realization > skepticism > rethinking (embracement or rejection). But the Guggenheim in Bilbao is especially interesting because it became positively embedded in the identity of the city's inhabitants, and re-introduced contemporary architecture into the realm of larger public discourse and a destination point for tourism.

Ultimately, it was not that buildings like the Guggenheim became superstars in the architectural, urban, and cultural landscapes of places that made the study interesting, but rather it was an attempt to understand the core prejudices toward visually unique and contemporary architectural interventions, and to illuminate how problematic the idea is that homogenous façades preserve places and generate good planning and architecture.

Buildings, along with cities and landscapes, as physical elements of the environment, are often seen as "fixed" or "unchangeable" and are as such highly contested, politicized objects that are used in defining, controlling, and defending an exclusive cultural narrative that goes beyond concerns about a building itself — and far beyond a new car or fashion trend. Thus, "perfect" architectural and landscape imagery of supposedly permanent places is utilized in an attempt to promulgate, propagate, and preserve a place, city, nation, or culture. It creates a fetishism and dependence upon "pictures" that results in a distorted ordering and organizing of physical space.

One result of the thesis, described in more depth in an article published in the Journal of Architectural Education[2], revealed that many people who objected to a new, contemporary library building in the city center of Münster, Germany, felt that it did not "fit in" and should be built outside the old medieval city ring and on the city's periphery, despite its function as a central piece of culture and public infrastructure. A few noted that it would destroy (the image of) the city. In other words, there was a direct connection between the judgment of the building and its geographic location. More precisely, for many, the building was seen as an "invader," since it had breached the borders of "their territory." In this particular case, it was defined as the old medieval city ring (wall). The close relationship between buildings, identity and territory became more apparent in the cognitive

maps drawn by the study participants in which artifacts, such as a large lake, which is outside the city ring, was "squeezed" into it. In other cognitive maps that included the ring and iconic buildings within it, nothing outside of the ring was drawn. It was clearly the border... the edge of territory, and it was evident that there was a complex relationship between buildings, people, place, and geographic space.

Thus, as one increases in scale from the individual and up to the scale of cities and nations, how one begins to define the edges of one's territory and identity (and what belongs in it) becomes increasingly problematic due to the complexity of relationships and intersecting identities and interests. Territory and a border define inside and outside, us and them, sameness and difference, but as the border grows larger and larger — both conceptually and physically — the edges begin to blur.

002 GOING HOME

Ordinary memory knows it so well that it sings, in all languages, of the sweetness of one's 'home sweet home'. Yet, the enclosed garden where the body hides its pains and joys is not a forbidden city. If it does not want to become a synonym for a terrible house arrest, separated from the living, the private space must know how to open itself up to the flow of people coming in and out, to be the passageway for a continual circulation, where objects, people, words, and ideas cross paths; for life is also about mobility, impatience for change, and relation to a plurality of others.[3]

"**A** merican architect seeks a small apartment to rent for 1 – 2 years. Tel. 0711/XXXXXXXX" This was the simple classified ad that appeared in the broadly read, local (German) newspaper *Stuttgarter Zeitung*. Within a day, the first offer to see an apartment had arisen. After knocking, the door opens, and the smiling face of a woman appears and immediately transforms into a stern face of disgust as she slams the door shut. Two days later, another call and another appointment to see an apartment is made. Minutes later, a knock on the door... it opens, and a frantic, "Uh... uh, the apartment is already rented!" can be heard as the door is slammed shut once again.

Walking along the Königsstrasse, Stuttgart's main pedestrian shopping street, a person spits and screams, "Go home!"

I would, but I haven't found an apartment, yet! the architect and saliva recipient thought to himself as people passed by, indifferent to the situation.

In a Frankfurt supermarket, seasonal vegetables are offered at a stand serviced and attended to by an employee. After the only other customer had been served and departing niceties exchanged, the employee turned around and began to shuffle around some objects, pretending to not have noticed the architect, even though he was standing right next to the last customer. "Excuse me," he proclaimed in German. "I would like some vegetables." No reaction… once, twice… nothing. In a final attempt with a raised voice, he then garnered the evil looks from passersby, but no reaction from the employee. As he walks away, baffled and frustrated, he glances back and sees another customer approaching the counter. She is served immediately, without summons.

Walking on the edge of Munich's Marienplatz, there is a sudden sharp pain in the architect's back, and he stumbles after an elbow is thrown. Accompanying the aggression is the phrase, "Go home, you piece of shit!"

I have used these incidents to open a lecture entitled, "The Politics of Pictures and Place" and show an image of a good-looking, young, white male in his thirties on the screen. I do not say that the picture is of "the" architect; it's just on the screen without captions or comments. As the story progresses, an additional, imaginary character and acquaintance of the architect expresses his disbelief and asks what he did after all of this. The architect replied, "Well, I decided that I really needed to start putting on clothes when I went out in public."

The mystery is lifted, smiles can be seen, and chuckles can be heard from the crowd. After revealing the truth about the photograph and incidents — that the photograph is a random person not known to me and that the stories are both true and personal — they admit being "deceived" by the image on the screen, and that stereotypical preconceptions about what an "American" looks like emerge so easily. Additionally, they reflect upon the fact that they allowed themselves to be "misled" by the neutral point of view used to deflect suspicions away from the (Asian-)American architect standing before them, who was introduced as having worked for years in Germany. Because the photograph was on the screen, it became more difficult to connect the dots and to conclude that the spit, screams, and elbows had anything to do with racism, despite the nature of the incidences and the fact that being Asian made it easier to be "visually stamped" and singled-out as an "Other" in the context of the three German cities.

I did not use these stories because I wanted to talk directly about racism, but rather about the politics of pictures and the powerful, yet sometimes very problematic, practice of misusing imagery (and vision) to judge and influence prejudices and perceptions. Even the resolution of the story was dependent on a very clear "picture" of a naked man going about his business in the crowded streets of Germany, though a photograph was not necessary. But that image was so clear that it also initially washes away any other critical questioning or ambiguity about an alternative reason for the incidences. The way we pass judgment on buildings is amazingly similar to how we initially judge people we don't know. We do it based on looks and first impressions. We use pictures, both real and mentally cached, to define, defend, and continue preconceptions and prejudices. The more powerful and cohesive the imagery, the more convincing is the story that accompanies it.

Ultimately, these incidences were especially interesting because they were so tightly connected to territory, but at very different scales and under very different contexts, just as the City Library in Münster. In the search for an apartment, the door(way) was an obvious and very much physical threshold between two types of spaces with a very clear inside and outside. Its definition is unambiguous, controllable, and finite. The parties involved and "ownership" of territory were legally defined. In the supermarket, the situation was more complex. The territory being occupied by the employee was not "under siege," but the transaction between the German supermarket employee and the foreign customer was a sort of proxy for national space that was being contested and controlled. The counter of fruits and vegetables offered the employee enough of a physical barrier and protection that defined territory. This gave her a sense of control, which in turn empowered her to ignore the architect and thus "defend national borders" within the privately controlled space of the supermarket. And finally, in the two incidents that took place in crowded public spaces, language was necessary to articulate and clarify what territory was being referenced. The context of a crowded place with others perceived as "one's own" empowered the spitter and elbow-thrower to attempt to expel an

"intruder" despite a lack of a physical barrier for protection or a physical/an immediate space to be expelled from. Their protection was the sheer number of perceived allies ("us") against the "Other." The architect had already penetrated the territorial boundaries, and "home" was a clear reference not to his apartment within the city, but rather to the outside of German borders, or more specifically — the country where "he was from," which was clearly implied as not possibly being Germany. We push and shove boundaries in an attempt to retain and protect territorial clarity, because when looking out, everything is nebulous, unknown, and foreign.

B.R.D.
ECHTERNACH

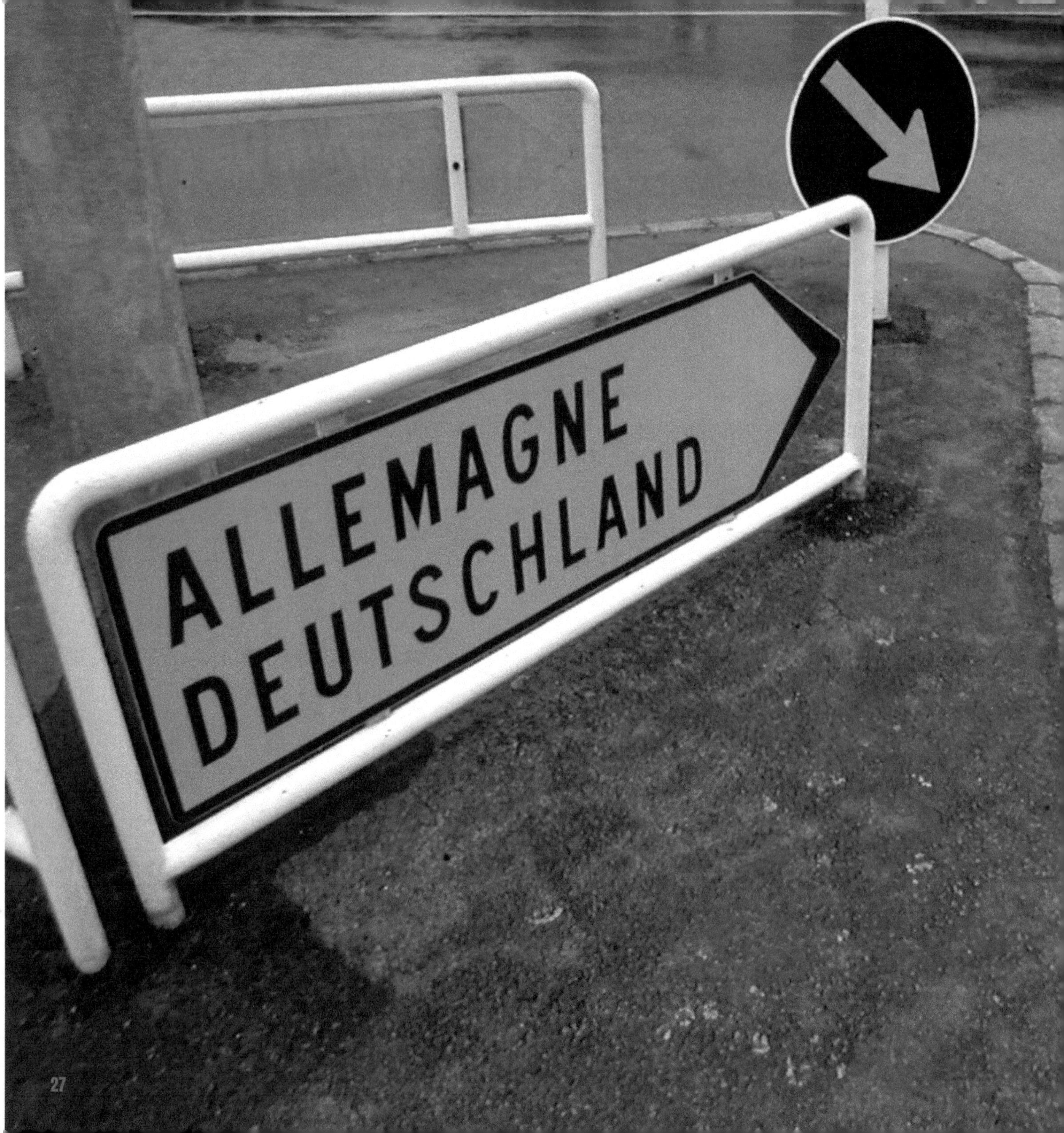
ALLEMAGNE
DEUTSCHLAND

003

PROXIMITY

We pass judgment on people, buildings and places with more intensive scrutiny when the foreign is "within our territory." It is well accepted that proxemics apply to individuals in public space, and that there are cultural differences in how large personal spaces are. But, are there proxemics for buildings as well? The Münster City Library, according to many, should have been built outside the city ring, and if Münster's city center were, for example, a UNESCO World Heritage Site, it could have very well been that the Library would not have been allowed to be built within it.

If one does not consider the visual appearances of a building, one could argue that there are certainly "functions" that are accepted or rejected based on proximity to the home or radius of action. Schools, bakeries, doctors' offices, and grocery stores are in general accepted, while nuclear power plants, heavy industry, and landfills ignite heated battles to keep such necessary functions of our society as far away as possible. Out of sight, out of mind. Intrusions are accepted as long as we perceive a direct, personal benefit, and no or little perceived "intrusion." The family with children look forward to a new school

being built near their home, while the childless couple, singles, or families with kids who have already left the nest are not looking forward to the noise of screaming and laughing kids, as well as increased vehicular traffic a school brings with it.

In Germany, the landmark decision made in 2011, following the nuclear meltdown in Japan at the Fukushima power plant, to move away from nuclear energy and to close down all reactors by 2021 has become in one particular aspect quite absurd: citizens and environmentalists who strongly supported and greatly influenced the decision are now protesting that the necessary wind turbines, solar panel farms, and power distribution lines should not be erected since they are a "blight" in the landscape… or at least "their" landscape.[4] Proximity makes us selfish.

35

CHANGE

"Wechselstelle" is a currency exchange office but translated literally means "place of change".

We have a peculiar relationship to "change." On the one hand, we tend to embrace new consumer technologies and products such as the latest smartphone, tablet, computer, and cars, but are resistant to things that we cannot so clearly see or things that are at a scale in which we deem to be "outside our personal realm." Changes which appear to be minor, like buying a smartphone, lead us to think that the changes are foreseeable (e.g., personal habits, convenience, and usage), while changes perceived on a larger scale have results and consequences that appear to bring uncertainty — e.g., moving away from fossil fuels or nuclear energy and toward renewable energy sources. Although the reasoning for major changes pertaining to renewable energy are solid and logical, there

is a strong resistance against making significant progress. While the initial, perceived "scale" of a change certainly influences our decisions and perceptions of change, when one begins to examine the complex results and ramification of decisions, one cannot help but see how the perceived size and scale are not determinants of the reach of consequences. Very small objects of communication technology, such as the smartphone, have radically changed our culture, and studies are revealing that they pose a serious threat to production workers, environment, and the health and cognitive skills of users, especially children and young adults. Earlier, but at a similar scale, the suburban house and the US Interstate system also radically transformed American culture in terms of the way Americans understand public space and public life.

Suburbia has contributed to an American society of fear and paranoia that has through a culture of isolation, subsequently, all but negated "public interaction/public life" by reducing it to a series of choreographed events in very controlled environments (supermarkets, malls, entertainment districts). At the core of

Suburbia are ideas that, as singular ones devoid of context and consequences, can be initially quite attractive. For example, while the single-family house with a garden is, for many, part of the American Dream, when it is multiplied by several million, and along with it the idea of individual freedom of movement through car ownership, the dream becomes a nightmare. This is not only due to the fact that the diffusion of people and infrastructure has major environmental impacts on resources and space, but also because the societal/social consequences of "isolation" are far-reaching — the negative often overtaking the positive.

For example, sending a child unaccompanied into public space was, and is, not the equivalent of sending the child into a war zone or "no-go" areas full of kidnappers and sexual offenders, as implied by incidents in the United States. Recently, a mother was charged with a child neglect felony for allowing her eight and five-year-old children to play at a playground 1.5 blocks away from their house unsupervised.[5] Since Americans have chased the dream of the suburban home and thereby conceded public space to the automobile, they have created huge swaths of barren, asphalt deserts, underscoring the isolation that the suburban house has created within cities and American society. Public spaces, if one can even call the expanses of roads and highways in American cities "public space," are now scary places, since they have become the unpopulated areas of "wilderness" — unknown and uncharted.

Josh Lauer of the University of New Hampshire wrote about the rise of the SUV in Suburbia of the 1980s as a rather strange phenomenon, since the "low-design" utilitarian vehicles did not correspond to the status and glamour obsessed time.[6] He asserts that the SUV became hugely popular as an extension of private space in order to protect one not from a traffic accident, but rather from a violent crime. In the 1990s, European luxury carmakers such as Mercedes, BMW, and even Porsche introduced their own sleekly designed, mid-sized versions of the SUV in order to regain some of the high-end market that it lost

through the American-made fortress-on-wheels.
So now, both in the US and Europe, the SUV offers
through the new design and luxury/accessory-
oriented models a typical "bigger-is-better"
status symbol, despite the fact that in Europe,
the unwieldy vehicles are too large for the often
smaller and narrower streets and parking spaces,
and the fuel prices on the "Old Continent" tend to
be more than twice as much as those in the US.

    Change is inevitable, but when we decide to
avoid it as opposed to consciously guide it, it creeps
up on us like a wild animal in the wilderness.

DIE GRENZE

JEDEN FREITAG, SAMSTAG UND SONNTAG DURCHGEHEND VON

8.00 bis 18.00 Uhr
GEÖFFNET

"The Border is open without breaks every Friday, Saturday, and Sunday from 8:00 to 18:00."

CHANGE 44

"Antiques"

005

TALK TO ME

ALTES

11   Bierspezialit

"old customs office/border control" restaurant

W hen I was in architecture school as an undergraduate, Postmodernism was still riding a peak, although within the schools of architecture, "the resistance" was certainly forming. "Beauty" was considered a bad word and direct "quotations" from the past moved to more free and expressionist uses of form as Deconstructivism emerged as the new kid on the block. But ultimately, both Postmodernism and Deconstructivism had been reduced to an idea about what buildings look like.

The idea that buildings could communicate with us through visual cues and symbolism assumed a shared understanding of the past and transformed buildings from places of experience into mere pictures in a storybook. And, it underscored the power of architecture and landscapes as political tools — in landscape and landmark/historic preservation, city planning, and urban design.

Linda Groat from the University of Michigan conducted one of the earliest studies that asked the question if architecture really can communicate a (clear) message.[7] The results of the study revealed that the "language" of form is for the most part too ambiguous, and the physical context in which a building stands is perhaps just as important or more important for one's ability to "get the message." This is both the power and problem in the "politics of buildings," since the generalities of form allow an easier appropriation through the elimination of detail, and the building without context excludes the "bigger picture" about a specific place and time. In both cases, it is about suppression of important information. Concentration on the exterior, visual characteristics of a building or landscape, and our initial perception, often without context, unfortunately predominates in general conversations and more importantly, and dangerously, in the political decision-making regarding our environment. It is unfortunate because it negates the idea of human experience in order to form a more complete understanding of the environment and the transformative and evolutionary nature of places before making decisions or policy.

Architecture and those who judge it are often too preoccupied with what it looks like — this can be seen in the way places are presented and described in professional magazines and journals — and less about "what it does." The latter is ultimately more interesting and relevant, since it has a much more profound effect on our ways of living and operating. "What things do" has little to do with "functions" in a building, but rather how architecture can change the way we perceive, feel, and operate in our environments in the most simple or profound ways. One simple example is a window — does it bring in light, is it a picture frame or does it bring to attention a certain way of seeing the landscape, the outside context or the inner world of a building's space? Is it at eye level so one can always see out "as one normally does," or can one only see the sky or perhaps even only feet as they stroll by? Is there a meaningful relationship between users, passersby, building, and context, or is it a purely arbitrary and formal one?

The obsession with the image as opposed to "content" can be seen in the planning on many college campuses. Administrators, students and visitors alike are blinded by the beauty of what they believe is created by the unified "looks" of the buildings, when in fact it is often the quality and human scale of urban or open spaces, well designed landscapes, and simple "amenities" such as benches and planters where students can sit and "populate" the campus. And instead of creating buildings with classrooms that have sufficient daylighting or spaces that, for example, open directly out to outdoor seminar or landscaped green spaces of the campus, objects for the photo-op and glossy brochures are created with little consideration for the actual quality of the interior spaces in regard to function and the human experience. Buildings can tell us revealing stories about the values of their creators and of a society — if we would only listen and learn.

If cultural identity is defined by a set of shared ideals, traditions, values, and beliefs, which determine a way of looking at the world, then it is also about shaping and regulating it through the establishment and "defense" of territory. For example, in the 1990s and a now resurgent discourse in Germany regarding immigrants and "integration" that has centered around the term "German Leitkultur" (literally translated: German lead culture) goes hand in hand with the preservation of territory and cultural identity. This utopian way of thinking, "evokes a nostalgia for a mythological past,... a stationary-state moral order and a hierarchical mode of social relating that is non-conflictual and harmonious. Territorialization is thus the cultural process of regulating space and social interaction. Laws, customs and territorial behavior are defenses against the Other, against the threat to personal security, self-esteem, self- and cultural-identity brought about by diversity."[8]

As our perception of the world becomes one of increasing complexity, unpredictability, pluralization and secularization, it is accompanied by an increasing number of discussions about identities — individuals, groups, nations — and how they are affected by so many things such as geography, technology, capital, politics, mobility, ethnicity, religion, and globalization. Identity seems most often discussed with the negative connotation of "losing" as opposed to "changing," "enriching," or "discovering." And, as seemingly endless possibilities arise out of the ever expanding wealth of and access to information and knowledge, globalization and the compression of time-space relations has led to a reactionary condition in which attempts are made to resist, control, or confine change to facets of our identities and lives that are seemingly the least threatening.

Ironically, it is precisely these reactionary practices of "preservation" that ultimately feed globalization through

tourism and the homogenization of places by suppressing or eliminating the variety and richness of a place one desires to "preserve." Preservation and the subsequent "branding" of places and identities might ensure a place's survival in a tourist economy through the exploitation of a few stereotypes, myths, and legends of dominant groups in power. However, it can also create museum-like environs that, with an unforgiving, straightjacket of rules and regulations designed to sell culture, rescind into meaninglessness or even obscure more pressing local and global conflicts and concerns. The politics of preservation (monuments, buildings, landscapes) typically exercised by most cities and nations are problematic for three reasons: 1) There is an overemphasis on what Alois Riegl calls "Age-value,"[9] 2) What is preserved is largely dependent upon what the dominant group deems appropriate for their "collective" narrative, and 3) It implies a very static understanding of a place and assumes there exists a monolithic culture.

The process of preservation and "branding" thus includes the careful compilation of an "inventory" of sellable artifacts, rituals, stories and environments that underscore the narrative history and legitimate the power and existence of the dominant group. Although components of the entire "inventory" ideally work in harmony with one another in order to "pull the show off," the connection to the physical environment is in many cases the most essential part of the equation, making clear why the appearance of the physical environment is inherently used as a political tool of identity formation and preservation.[10] The contradictions that may arise are willingly swept away at the discretion of the "culture police." For example, while many would question the authenticity of a Dutch cheese festival in a Walmart parking lot in downtown Jackson, Mississippi, the presence of global corporations such as MacDonald's, H&M, Nike, and Starbuck's in reconstructed 16th century merchant's buildings in the core of Münster do not raise an eyebrow. The ritual represented

by the cheese festival loses meaning without a "convincing" context, while a powerfully constructed "stage" can overshadow any contradictions or flaws in the story. It is the context for Culture consumption that must be right. In other words, there is a great deal of value placed on what is sold as an "authentic" environment or event in order to enhance and make the experience memorable.

In the USA, one needs only to look at the social isolation and monotony embodied in the American suburbs and the surging interest in the nostalgic principles of New Urbanism, as well as the gentrification, re-construction, and regeneration of the dilapidated downtowns of Mainstreet, USA, in order to understand the yearning and search for a no-longer-existent identity and place of yesteryear behind the quaint, reconstructed facades of history. The nostalgia embedded within the narratives of history can erase the realities of the present and distort the past, since the memories themselves are generalized, edited, and purified. The built and physical environment serves to preserve the narrative/myth/story upon which social values, political ideologies, and identities can be anchored in order to maintain power and the status quo. It is a way of providing stability and belonging, and it is the belief that these appearances actually "speak the truth" or that they can resurrect the past, which make the built and physical environment such powerful, political tools. "Nation-building(s)" need maintenance.

TERRITORY 72

HOW TO DEFEND A BORDER

WITH A SAUSAGE

The "Nürnberger Rostbratwurst" (Nuremburg Roasted Bratwurst) was put under the European Union's Geographical Indications Protection in 2003. [11] Thus, in order to carry the name "Nürnberger Rostbratwurst," the sausage must comply to production techniques and ingredients and most importantly, be produced within the borders of Nuremburg, the largest city in the Bavarian region of Franconia. The main raw ingredients: pork, marjoram, pepper, salt, and sheep casings must not come from Nuremburg — and in fact come from places as far away as India, Brazil, Vietnam (pepper), Iran, Iraq (casings) and Denmark (pork). The real absurdity lies in the territorial exclusion. The local or regional, fourth-generation Franconian farmer and butcher, who raises and slaughters her/his own pigs, sheep, etc., but happens to be on the wrong side of the city border — whether one centimeter or one kilometer (or 5000 for that matter) — is forbidden to name her/his product "Nürnberger Rostbratwurst," despite the fact that the product is arguably more "authentic" than the sausages mass-produced in factories within the city limits. Blood and soil won't save you from sausage-ism.

"Grenzpunkt" = border point | Can a line be a point?

008

IN BETWEEN

If right is France, left is Germany... where am I now? As I move, the conditions
don't change — it's as if the "eyes of Mona Lisa" follow me around the room,
denying access to beyond the "inbetween."

Driving north, the static emanating out of the car radio gradually transforms into a familiar melody; a pop tune by an American group, or perhap s a British one (somehow those English manage to "hide" their accents while banging out the lyrics to a catchy tune). Gradually, there is once again static as the automatic "seek" function takes control of the primitive, factory-installed radio in my 1992 Opel Corsa. There is suddenly a German DJ belting out the weekend cultural events in Maastricht, The Netherlands, before introducing the "hottest" experimental, electronic music coming out of Japan. The clarity once again fades into static, and after a few seconds of "seeking," the radio magically settles on a Dutch talk show broadcasting out of Venlo. The signs along the road are changing from German to Dutch and back to German and from yellow to blue to green and back to yellow, although the symbols stay essentially the same, aside from the ubiquitous Dutch windmill, which can be seen on every sign presenting national speed limits on highways, country roads, and city streets.

There is a strange atmosphere of "placeless-ness" which dominates the surface scenery — a sense of desertion and stasis. The changes in the built environment indicate that I am driving along and continually crossing a border between two nations. A border, which at one time more "clearly" demarcated territory, "inside" and "outside" or "us" and "them," through the attempt to physically control it with fences and checkpoints. Signage and the artifacts of the built environment still attest to its existence, but the land(scape) is essentially the same out the front windshield and the left, right, and rear windows, and thus tells a different story. It reveals the artificiality of borders and their socially and politically constructed nature. Perhaps the radio begins to reveal the changing nature of these borders and the potential and conflicts that are emerging in the blurring of edges and boundaries, both real and virtual.

IN BETWEEN '99

CONFLICT

Order, conformity and social homogeneity, perceived as virtuous, are believed to be strengthened by the securing of boundaries, which "brings into being a morally superior condition to one where there is mixing because mixing (of social groups and of diverse activities in space) carries the threat of contamination and a challenge to hegemonic values. Thus, spatial boundaries are in part moral boundaries. Spatial separations symbolize a moral order... "[12]

The land, absent of human occupation, is like an empty canvas. Although such an empty canvas arguably no longer exists, such land is a neutral space. However, it loses that neutrality as soon as the hand or eye of a human sees it, touches it, changes it, occupies it, and attempts to "capture" it. It then becomes landscape — a receptacle for human experience, a framework, which includes buildings that are built, mountains moved, and stories told. It is space and everything contained within it. It is anything but neutral. The layers of "paint" (imagined, conceived, or carried out) reveal stories of power and ownership, of control and exclusion, and of peace and hope. The "language" of the landscape is often itself ambiguous, but the representations of landscape are seldom transcripts of this ambiguity. They are, more often than not, "skewed interpretations" in a political arsenal in the battle for power and identity. Thus, it is often not the landscape itself, but rather the distorted perceptions and representations of the landscape that coerce us into action or concordance and feelings of attachment or disengagement. The landscape is both an object of desire and a banal part of our everyday lives. It is an appropriated part of our identity, and the stories it tells are dependent on both our own frame of reference, as well as that of the "Other." The physical spaces we inhabit can merge and unify or segregate and suppress. The environment is an essential compo-

nent of our experience as the confluence of place, space, identity and power.

The landscape is a concrete, tangible, or at least seemingly tangible, element that is presented either as a collective product or a pre-existing artifact/condition that everyone can comprehend and experience simultaneously. Albeit, perceptions vary, but it is the proposed possibility that in our physical environment, there exists an objective, concrete, and graspable, shared meaning or truth, which ultimately makes the landscape so potent and powerful. In order to make use of this power, it is typically only the unique (or asserted unique) landscape that is perpetuated as a national treasure/cultivated artifact. These landscapes — depicted in paintings, photographs, and advertisements — have been and are often utilized as tools for defining product, corporate, or national identity. The process of appropriation and claiming of the land(scape) as one's own is problematic because it presumes the existence of culture before environment, a right of "ownership" based on occupation, and the assumption that there is a point at which one land(scape) ends and another begins.

SMUDGING

"As people move with their meanings, and as meanings find ways of traveling even when people stay put, territories cannot really contain cultures. And even as one accepts that culture is socially acquired and organized, the assumption that it is homogeneously distributed within collectivities becomes problematic, when we see how their members' experiences and biographies differ."[13]

CHANGE

As our world becomes more intimately connected, perhaps one challenge of the future is rooted in the understanding of culture, our land and our cityscapes as interwoven, continually metamorphosing entities that embrace a dynamic definition of a local and global collective that is not bounded by geographical or national space. It is a way of seeing and transforming culture from a product of the past into a potential for the future. Borders and barriers will probably continue to exist — political, economic, and linguistic amongst others, but is a continual blurring possible or desirable? For example, will the radio stations and the voices of DJs continue to flicker in and out between German, French, Dutch, Luxembourgish, Flemish, Turkish or even Chinese? There are no clear signals on the margin... and that is perhaps the way it should be.

The images document a few of the new conditions along the border terrain that was once a more highly contested edge. Along the western border of Germany, history and commemoration are addressed with varying importance in various forms and fashions on some sites, while on others, the practices of everyday life and the sometimes strange juxtapositions that they bring with them are allowed to flourish. The photographs and essays attempt to bring to light the new (and old) conflicts that have arisen under the current conditions and contexts of the European Union. The circumstances surrounding the homosexual Dutch-German couple mentioned in 001 revealed how farcical the proverbial line in the sand can be, and how laws that varied from nation to nation could be subverted by moving just one millimeter from one side to the other. Simultaneously, a border for others who don't have the privilege of international mobility can be life-threatening or lifesaving, depending on which side of that border one stands, and perhaps how far away it is.

With the elimination of the internal European borders, an extraordinary opportunity has arisen in which "lines" turn into "smudges," "clarity" into "ambiguity," and "fringes" into "centers." The snapshots from Germany and its neighbors reveal how and to what extent the new "borderless" conditions within Europe are being negotiated, and are perhaps most valuable in illuminating the artificially constructed nature of the boundaries we set. The images and texts also attempt to expose the hidden side of national identities that conflict with those promulgated in political and cultural rhetoric, stereotypes and tourist brochures — that of simplicity, modesty... and sublime banality.

011 NOTES

[1] Frank Gehry's iconic Guggenheim Museum in Bilbao helped transform a downtrodden and dilapidated city into a tourists' destination of art and culture. Afterwards, countless cities attempted to recreate this effect by hiring "star architects" and building extravagant museums and "houses of culture."

[2] Song, Linn. "The Muenster City Library: The Politics of Identity and Place." *Journal of Architectural Education* Volume 60, Issue 3 (2007): pp. 12-20.

[3] See Grasskamp, Walter, *Unerwuenschte Monumente* [Unwanted Monuments]: *Moderne Kunst im Stadtraum*, 2. Auflage (Munich: Verlag Silke Schreiber, 1993), p.148. Grasskamp comments on the state of public art in the realm of the city.

[4] Dieter Hanisch, "Ein realer Kampf gegen Windmühlen," *Zeit Online*, November 30th, 2011, http://www.zeit.de/politik/deutschland/2011-11/windkraft-protest-schleswig-holstein

[5] Laura Halm, "Mom Speaks Out About Neglect Charges," WCYB/WEMT Bristol, VA, June 8th, 2012, http://www.wcyb.com/Mom-Speaks-Out-About-Neglect-Charges/-/14590664/15240294/-/a4vswuz/-/index.html.

"Johnson City police charge mom with neglect after kids go missing from playground," *Johnson City Press*, Johnson City, TN, June 8th, 2012, http://www.johnsoncitypress.com/News/article.php?id=100729.

[6] Lauer, Josh. "Driven to Extremes: Fear of crime and the rise of the sport utility vehicle in the United States." *Crime Media Culture* Vol. 1(2) (2005): 149-168.

[7] Groat, L. and Canter, D. (1979). "Does Post-Modern Architecture Communicate?" *Progressive Architecture*, December, 84-87.

[8] Altman, Rapoport and Wohlwill, ed., *Human Behavior and Environment, Advances in Theory and Research, Vol. 4 Environment and Culture* (New York: Plenum Press, 1980), p. 181

[9] Riegl, Alois, "The Modern Cult of Monuments: Its Character and Its Origin", transl. by Kurt W. Forster and Diane Ghirardo in *Oppositions Reader*, Michael Hays, ed., pp. 621-651 (New York: Princeton Architectural Press, 1998)

[10] Boyer, M. Christine, "Cities for Sale" in *Variations on a Theme Park; The New American City and the End of Public Space*, Michael Sorkin, ed. (New York: Hill and Wang, 1999), pp. 202-203.

[11] "Geographical Indications and Designations of Origin," Council Regulation (EC) No 510/2006 of 20 March 2006 on the protection of geographical indications and designations of origin for agricultural products and foodstuffs, http://europa.eu/legislation_summaries/internal_market/businesses/intellectual_property/l66044_en.htm.

"Original Nürnberger Rostbratwürste," accessed August 1st, 2012, http://www.nuernberger-bratwuerste.de/erfahren/nuernberger-bratwurst.

[12] Sibley, David, *Geographies of Exclusion: Society and Difference in the West* (New York: Routledge, 1995), p. 39.

[13] Hannerz, Ulf, Transnational Connections; Culture, People, Places (London: Routledge, 1996), p. 8.

012 IMAGES

All photographs are by Linn Song in 2002 & 2003.

COVER
NL-Bourtange – DE-Neuheede

TITLE PAGE
DE-Charlottenpolder

000
DE-Neuenburg am Rhein – FR-Chalampé
DE-B402 – NL-N37

001
BE-Köpfchen
NL-Vaals
DE-Rütenbrock
FR-Lauterbourg
NL-Bellingwedde – DE-Duenebroek
FR- Petite-Roselle – DE-Großrossel
DE-Nordhorn
FR-Merten
NL-Glane
FR-Wissembourg – DE-Windhof

002
DE-Bisten – FR-Merten
DE-Dornhegge – NL-Enschede
DE-Neuenburg am Rhein
FR-Sarreguimines – DE-Habkirchen
LU-Echternach
LU-Echternach
DE-Rheinau

003
DE-Bildchen
DE-Hornbach
FR-Scheibenhard
DE-Waldfeucht
DE-Saarbrücken
DE-Springbiel
DE-Bisten – FR-Merten
FR-Petite-Roselle
NL-Coevorden – DE-Eschebruegge
NL-Bourtange – DE-Neuheede

004

FR-Sarreguimines – DE-Hanweiler
LU-Wormeldange
DE-Saarbrücken
BE-Köpfchen
FR-Wissembourg – DE-Windhof
DE-Nordhorn
NL-Polsterholt
DE-Nassweiler
NL-Losser – DE-Harning
NL-Gendringen
FR-Lauterbourg
NL-Gendringen
DE-Koepfchen – BE-Hauser
DE-Nordhorn

005

DE-Rheinau
DE-Rheinau
FR-Sarreguimines – DE-Hanweiler
NL-Ubbergen
DE-Nordhorn
DE-Nordhorn
NL-Gendrigen
DE-Rheinau – FR-Gambsheim
BE-Köfchen
NL-Zwilbroek
FR-Sarreguimines – DE-Habkirchen
FR-Scheibenhard A35
FR-Scheibenhard A35

006

NL-Bourtange – DE-Neuheede
DE-Nassweiler
DE-Nordhorn
DE-Bisten – FR-Merten
LU-Wormeldange
BE-Köpfchen
FR-Merten
DE-Neuenburg am Rhein
NL-Vaals
NL-Laar – DE-Wolde
FR-Huningue
DE-Balderhaar

007

DE-Sasbach
DE-Bisten – FR-Merten
DE-Bisten – FR-Merten
DE-Bisten – FR-Merten
NL-Bad Nieuweschans A7
DE-Springbiel
FR-Sarreguimines –DE-Habkirchen
DE-Baldehaar
NL-Bourtange – DE-Neuheede
DE-Springbiel

008

FR-ScheibenhardA35
FR-Sarreguimines – DE-Habkirchen
DE-Rhede
DE-Sasbach – FR-Markolsheim
NL-Beek/Ubbergen
NL-Gendringen
DE-Neuenburg am Rhein
DE-Nordhorn
NL-Middendorf – DE-Twist
NL-Beek/Ubbergen
NL-Bad Nieuweschans A7
DE-Sasbach – FR-Markolsheim

009

DE-Breisach
NL-Achterin
NL-Achterin
NL-Bellingwedde – DE-Duenebroek
NL-Laar – DE-Wolde
DE-Charlottenpolder
NL-Schoonebeck – DE-Emlichheim
NL-Middendorf – DE-Twist

010

NL-Vaals
NL-Laar – DE-Wolde
FR-Sarreguimines – DE-Hanweiler
BE-Losheimersgraben
NL-Achterin

CPSIA information can be obtained
at www.ICGtesting.com
Printed in the USA
BVHW021720301120
594526BV00012B/504